The Poetry Of Robert Burns

An Introduction

Poetry is a fascinating use of language. With almost a million words at its command it is not surprising that these Isles have produced some of the most beautiful, moving and descriptive verse through the centuries. In this series we look at individual poets who have shaped and influenced their craft and cement their place in our heritage.

Many nations have produced outstanding poets who they would gladly have represent their Culture. But can any Nation say they have an equivalent of Robbie Burns? Rabbie. The Ploughman Poet. The Bard (Of Scotland). This one poet is indelibly linked and intertwined with the culture and people of Scotland. His life, loves, politics, verse and songs speak as them and for them.

From humble roots, the eldest son of seven born in 1759 to parents, both from tenant farming stock, the family endured both hardship and poverty. Burns endured the test and began to write first at 15 and to publish his first volume some two years later.

He wrote in both true Scottish, dialect and English as well as turning his hand to song. Politically he was an inspiration to both liberalism and socialism as well as a Scottish parliament. His unique ability enabled him to appeal to all and quite rightly to be viewed as the National poet.

As well as creating his own great works he was also an avid collector of Scottish Folk Songs preserving for posterity the works of others.

However his own life was short dying at the young age of only 37. What further greatness would have lain before him is impossible to say. But, poetically, on the day of his death his son, Maxwell was born.

His fame today is worldwide and celebrated in January each year with the Traditional Burns night. Each New Years Eve friends and families the world over link arms to 'Auld Lang Syne', giving immortality to his words and aims.

As former Secretary General of the United Nations, Kofi Annan says: Burn's *poems dignify and illuminate the struggle faced by the vast majority of the world's population today.*

In this slim volume the very best of his work is brought to you.

Many of the poems are also available as an audiobook from our sister company Portable Poetry. Many samples are at our youtube channel http://www.youtube.com/user/PortablePoetry?feature=mhee The full volume can be purchased from iTunes, Amazon and other digital stores and is read for you by Gordon Kennedy

Index

THE SELKIRT GRACE
Some hae meat, and canna eat
And some wad eat that want it;
But we hae meat and we can eat,

And sae the Lord be Thankit.

AULD LANG SYNE
Should auld acquaintance be forgot,
And never brought to min?
Should auld acquaintance be forgot,
And auld lang syne!

For auld lang syne, my dear,
For auld lang syne.
We'll tak a cup o' kindness yet,
For auld lang syne.

We twa hae run about the braes,
And pou'd the gowans fine;
But we've wander'd mony a weary foot,
Sin' auld lang syne.

We twa hae paidled I' the burn,
From morning sun till dine;
But seas between us braid hae roar'd
Sin' auld lang syne.

And there's a hand, my trusty fiere!
And gie's a hand o' thine!
And we'll tak a right gude-willie waught,
For auld lang syne.

And surely ye'll be your pint stowp!
And surely I'll be mine!
And we'll tak a cup o'kindness yet,
For auld lang syne.

TAM O' SHANTER, A TALE
When chapman billies leave the street,
And drouthy neibors, neibors, meet;
As market-days are wearing late,
And folk begin to tak the gate,

While we sit bousing at the nappy,
An' getting fou and unco happy,
We think na on the lang Scots miles,
The mosses, waters, slaps and stiles,
That lie between us and our hame,
Where sits our sulky, sullen dame,
Gathering her brows like gathering storm,
Nursing her wrath to keep it warm.

This truth fand honest Tam o' Shanter,
As he frae Ayr ae night did canter:
(Auld Ayr, wham ne'er a town surpasses,
For honest men and bonnie lasses).

O Tam! had'st thou but been sae wise,
As ta'en thy ain wife Kate's advice!
She tauld thee weel thou was a skellum,
A blethering, blustering, drunken blellum;
That frae November till October,
Ae market-day thou was na sober;
That ilka melder wi' the Miller,
Thou sat as lang as thou had siller;
That ev'ry naig was ca'd a shoe on
The Smith and thee gat roarin' fou on;
That at the Lord's house, even on Sunday,
Thou drank wi' Kirkton Jean till Monday,
She prophesied that late or soon,
Thou would be found, deep drown'd in Doon,
Or catch'd wi' warlocks in the mirk,
By Alloway's auld, haunted kirk.

Ah, gentle dames! it gars me greet,
To think how mony counsels sweet,
How mony lengthen'd, sage advices,
The husband frae the wife despises!

But to our tale: Ae market night,
Tam had got planted unco right,
Fast by an ingle, bleezing finely,
Wi reaming swats, that drank divinely;
And at his elbow, Souter Johnny,
His ancient, trusty, droughty crony:

Tam lo'ed him like a very brither;
They had been fou for weeks thegither.
The night drave on wi' sangs and clatter;
And aye the ale was growing better:
The Landlady and Tam grew gracious,
Wi' favours secret, sweet, and precious:
The Souter tauld his queerest stories;
The Landlord's laugh was ready chorus:
The storm without might rair and rustle,
Tam did na mind the storm a whistle.

Care, mad to see a man sae happy,
E'en drown'd himsel amang the nappy.
As bees flee hame wi' lades o' treasure,
The minutes wing'd their way wi' pleasure:
Kings may be blest, but Tam was glorious,
O'er a' the ills o' life victorious!

But pleasures are like poppies spread,
You seize the flow'r, its bloom is shed;
Or like the snow falls in the river-
A moment white--then melts for ever;
Or like the Borealis race,
That flit ere you can point their place;
Or like the Rainbow's lovely form
Evanishing amid the storm.--
Nae man can tether Time nor Tide,
The hour approaches Tam maun ride;
That hour, o' night's black arch the key-stane,
That dreary hour he mounts his beast in;
And sic a night he taks the road in,
As ne'er poor sinner was abroad in.

The wind blew as 'twad blawn its last;
The rattling show'rs rose on the blast;
The speedy gleams the darkness swallow'd;
Loud, deep, and lang, the thunder bellow'd:
That night, a child might understand,
The deil had business on his hand.

Weel-mounted on his grey mare, Meg,
A better never lifted leg,

Tam skelpit on thro' dub and mire,
Despising wind, and rain, and fire;
Whiles holding fast his gude blue bonnet,
Whiles crooning o'er some auld Scots sonnet,
Whiles glow'ring round wi' prudent cares,
Lest bogles catch him unawares;
Kirk-Alloway was drawing nigh,
Whare ghaists and houlets nightly cry.

By this time he was cross the ford,
Where in the snaw the chapman smoor'd;
And past the birks and meikle stane,
Where drunken Charlie brak's neck-bane;
And thro' the whins, and by the cairn,
Where hunters fand the murder'd bairn;
And near the thorn, aboon the well,
Where Mungo's mither hang'd hersel'.
Before him Doon pours all his floods,
The doubling storm roars thro' the woods,
The lightnings flash from pole to pole,
Near and more near the thunders roll,
When, glimmering thro' the groaning trees,
Kirk-Alloway seem'd in a bleeze,
Thro' ilka bore the beams were glancing,
And loud resounded mirth and dancing.

Inspiring bold John Barleycorn!
What dangers thou canst make us scorn!
Wi' tippenny, we fear nae evil;
Wi' usquabae, we'll face the devil!
The swats sae ream'd in Tammie's noddle,
Fair play, he car'd na deils a boddle,
But Maggie stood, right sair astonish'd,
Till, by the heel and hand admonish'd,
She ventur'd forward on the light;
And, wow! Tam saw an unco sight!

Warlocks and witches in a dance:
Nae cotillon, brent new frae France,
But hornpipes, jigs, strathspeys, and reels,
Put life and mettle in their heels.
A winnock-bunker in the east,

There sat auld Nick, in shape o' beast;
A touzie tyke, black, grim, and large,
To gie them music was his charge:
He screw'd the pipes and gart them skirl,
Till roof and rafters a' did dirl.--
Coffins stood round, like open presses,
That shaw'd the Dead in their last dresses;
And by some devilish cantraip sleight
Each in its cauld hand held a light.
By which heroic Tam was able
To note upon the haly table,
A murderer's banes, in gibbet-airns;
Twa span-lang, wee, unchristen'd bairns;
A thief, new-cutted frae a rape,
Wi' his last gasp his gabudid gape;
Five tomahawks, wi' blude red-rusted:
Five scimitars, wi' murder crusted;
A garter which a babe had strangled:
A knife, a father's throat had mangled.
Whom his ain son of life bereft,
The gray hairs yet stack to the heft;
Wi' mair of horrible and awfu',
Which even to name wad be unlawfu'.

As Tammie glowr'd, amaz'd, and curious,
The mirth and fun grew fast and furious;
The Piper loud and louder blew,
The dancers quick and quicker flew,
The reel'd, they set, they cross'd, they cleekit,
Till ilka carlin swat and reekit,
And coost her duddies to the wark,
And linkit at it in her sark!

Now Tam, O Tam! had they been queans,
A' plump and strapping in their teens!
Their sarks, instead o' creeshie flainen,
Been snaw-white seventeen hunder linen!--
Thir breeks o' mine, my only pair,
That ance were plush o' guid blue hair,
I wad hae gien them off my hurdies,
For ae blink o' the bonie burdies!

But wither'd beldams, auld and droll,
Rigwoodie hags wad spean a foal,
Louping an' flinging on a crummock.
I wonder did na turn thy stomach.

But Tam kent what was what fu' brawlie:
There was ae winsome wench and walie
That night enlisted in the core,
Lang after kent on Carrick shore;
(For mony a beast to dead she shot,
And perish'd mony a bonnie boat,
And shook baith meikle corn and bear,
And kept the country-side in fear);
Her cutty sark, o' Paisley harn,
That while a lassie she had worn,
In longitude tho' sorely scanty,
It was her best, and she was vauntie.
Ah! little ken'd thy reverend grannie,
That sark she coft for her wee Nannie,
Wi twa pund Scots ('twas a' her riches),
Wad ever grac'd a dance of witches!

But here my Muse her wing maun cour,
Sic flights are far beyond her pow'r;
To sing how Nannie lap and flang,
(A souple jade she was and strang),
And how Tam stood, like ane bewitch'd,
And thought his very een enrich'd:
Even Satan glowr'd, and fidg'd fu' fain,
And hotch'd and blew wi' might and main:
Till first ae caper, syne anither,
Tam tint his reason a' thegither,
And roars out, "Weel done, Cutty-sark!"
And in an instant all was dark:
And scarcely had he Maggie rallied.
When out the hellish legion sallied.

As bees bizz out wi' angry fyke,
When plundering herds assail their byke,
As open pussie's mortal foes,
When, pop! she starts before their nose;
As eager runs the market-crowd,

When "Catch the thief!" resounds aloud;
So Maggie runs, the witches follow,
Wi' mony an eldritch skreich and hollow.

Ah, Tam! Ah, Tam! thou'll get thy fairin!
In hell, they'll roast thee like a herrin!
In vain thy Kate awaits thy comin!
Kate soon will be a woefu' woman!
Now, do thy speedy-utmost, Meg,
And win the key-stone o' the brig:
There, at them thou thy tail may toss,
A running stream they darena cross.
But ere the key-stane she could make,
The fient a tail she had to shake!
For Nannie, far before the rest,
Hard upon noble Maggie prest,
And flew at Tam wi' furious ettle;
But little wist she Maggie's mettle!
Ae spring brought off her master hale,
But left behind her ain grey tail:

The carlin claught her by the rump,
And left poor Maggie scarce a stump.

Now, wha this tale o' truth shall read,
Each man and mother's son, take heed:
Whene'er to drink you are inclin'd,
Or cutty-sarks rin in your mind,
Think ye may buy the joys o'er dear;
Remember Tam o' Shanter's mare.

THE COTTER'S SATURDAY NIGHT
My lov'd, my honour'd, much respected friend!
No mercenary bard his homage pays;
With honest pride, I scorn each selfish end,
My dearest meed, a friend's esteem and praise:
To you I sing, in simple Scottish lays,
The lowly train in life's sequester'd scene,
The native feelings strong, the guileless ways,
What Aiken in a cottage would have been-

Ah! tho' his worth unknown, far happier there I ween!

November chill blaws loud wi' angry sough;
The short'ning winter-day is near a close;
The miry beasts retreating frae the pleugh;
The black'ning trains o' craws to their repose:
The toil-worn Cotter frae his labour goes,
This night his weekly moil is at an end,
Collects his spades, his mattocks, and his hoes,
Hoping the morn in ease and rest to spend,
And weary, o'er the moor, his course does homeward bend.

At length his lonely cot appears in view,
Beneath the shelter of an aged tree;
Th' expectant wee-things, toddlin, stacher through
To meet their Dad, wi' flichterin noise and glee.
His wee bit ingle, blinkin bonnilie,
His clean hearth-stane, his thrifty wifie's smile,
The lisping infant prattling on his knee,
Does a' his weary kiaugh and care beguile,
An' makes him quite forget his labour an' his toil.

Belyve, the elder bairns come drapping in,
At service out, amang the farmers roun';
Some ca' the pleugh, some herd, some tentie rin
A cannie errand to a neibor town:
Their eldest hope, their Jenny, woman-grown,
In youthfu' bloom-love sparkling in her e'e
Comes hame, perhaps to shew a braw new gown,
Or deposite her sair-won penny-fee,
To help her parents dear, if they in hardship be.

With joy unfeign'd, brothers and sisters meet,
And each for other's weelfare kindly speirs:
The social hours, swift-wing'd, unnotic'd fleet:
Each tells the uncos that he sees or hears.
The parents, partial, eye their hopeful years;
Anticipation forward points the view;
The mother, wi' her needle and her sheers,
Gars auld claes look amaist as weel's the new;
The father mixes a' wi' admonition due.

Their master's and their mistress' command,
The younkers a' are warned to obey;
And mind their labours wi' an eydent hand,
And ne'er, tho' out o' sight, to jauk or play;
"And O! be sure to fear the Lord alway,
An' mind your duty, duly, morn and night;
Lest in temptation's path ye gang astray,
Implore His counsel and assisting might:
They never sought in vain that sought the Lord aright."

But hark! a rap comes gently to the door;
Jenny, wha kens the meaning o' the same,
Tells how a neibor lad came o'er the moor,
To do some errands, and convoy her hame.
The wily mother sees the conscious flame
Sparkle in Jenny's e'e, and flush her cheek;
With heart-struck anxious care, enquires his name,
While Jenny hafflins is afraid to speak;
Weel-pleased the mother hears, it's nae wild, worthless rake.

Wi' kindly welcome, Jenny brings him ben;
A strappin youth; he takes the mother's eye;
Blythe Jenny sees the visit's no ill ta'en;
The father cracks of horses, pleughs, and kye.
The youngster's artless heart o'erflows wi' joy,
But blate an' laithfu', scarce can weel behave;
The mother, wi' a woman's wiles, can spy
What makes the youth sae bashfu' and sae grave,
Weel-pleased to think her bairn's respected like the lave

O happy love! where love like this is found:
O heart-felt raptures! bliss beyond compare!
I've paced much this weary, mortal round,
And sage experience bids me this declare,
"If Heaven a draught of heavenly pleasure spare
One cordial in this melancholy vale,
'Tis when a youthful, loving, modest pair
In other's arms breathe out the tender tale,
Beneath the milk-white thorn that scents the evening gale."

Is there, in human form, that bears a heart
A wretch! a villain! lost to love and truth

That can, with studied, sly, ensnaring art,
Betray sweet Jenny's unsuspecting youth?
Curse on his perjur'd arts! dissembling smooth!
Are honour, virtue, conscience, all exil'd?
Is there no pity, no relenting ruth,
Points to the parents fondling o'er their child?
Then paints the ruin'd maid, and their distraction wild?

But now the supper crowns their simple board,
The halesome parritch, chief of Scotia's food;
The sowpe their only hawkie does afford,
That, 'yont the hallan snugly chows her cood:
The dame brings forth, in complimental mood,
To grace the lad, her weel-hain'd kebbuck, fell;
And aft he's prest, and aft he ca's it guid:
The frugal wifie, garrulous, will tell
How t'was a towmond auld, sin' lint was i' the bell.

The cheerfu' supper done, wi' serious face,
They, round the ingle, form a circle wide;
The sire turns o'er, with patriarchal grace,
The big ha'bible, ance his father's pride:
His bonnet rev'rently is laid aside,
His lyart haffets wearing thin and bare;
Those strains that once did sweet in Zion glide,
He wales a portion with judicious care;
And "Let us worship God!" he says with solemn air.

They chant their artless notes in simple guise;
They tune their hearts, by far the noblest aim;
Perhaps Dundee's wild warbling measures rise;
Or plaintive Martyrs, worthy of the name;
Or noble Elgin beets the heav'nward flame;
The sweetest far of Scotia's holy lays:
Compar'd with these, Italian trills are tame;
The tickl'd ears no heart-felt raptures raise;
Nae unison hae they with our Creator's praise.

The priest-like father reads the sacred page,
How Abram was the friend of God on high;
Or Moses bade eternal warfare wage
With Amalek's ungracious progeny;

Or how the royal bard did groaning lie
Beneath the stroke of Heaven's avenging ire;
Or Job's pathetic plaint, and wailing cry;
Or rapt Isaiah's wild, seraphic fire;
Or other holy seers that tune the sacred lyre.

Perhaps the Christian volume is the theme,
How guiltless blood for guilty man was shed;
How He, who bore in Heaven the second name,
Had not on earth whereon to lay His head;
How His first followers and servants sped;
The precepts sage they wrote to many a land:
How he, who lone in Patmos banished,
Saw in the sun a mighty angel stand,
And heard great Bab'lon's doom pronounced by Heaven's command.

Then, kneeling down to Heaven's Eternal King,
The saint, the father, and the husband prays:
Hope "springs exulting on triumphant wing,"
That thus they all shall meet in future days,
There ever bask in uncreated rays,
No more to sigh, or shed the bitter tear,
Together hymning their Creator's praise,
In such society, yet still more dear;
While circling Time moves round in an eternal sphere

Compared with this, how poor Religion's pride,
In all the pomp of method and of art;
When men display to congregations wide
Devotion's ev'ry grace, except the heart!
The Power, incensed, the pageant will desert,
The pompous strain, the sacerdotal stole;
But haply, in some cottage far apart,
May hear, well-pleased, the language of the soul;
And in His Book of Life the inmates poor enrol.

Then homeward all take off their several way;
The youngling cottagers retire to rest:
The parent-pair their secret homage pay,
And proffer up to Heav'n the warm request,
That he who stills the raven's clamorous nest,
And decks the lily fair in flowery pride,

Would, in the way His wisdom sees the best,
For them and for their little ones provide;
But chiefly in their hearts with grace divine preside.

From scenes like these, old Scotia's grandeur springs,
That makes her loved at home, revered abroad:
Princes and lords are but the breath of kings,
"An honest man's the noblest work of God;"
And certes, in fair virtue's heavenly road,
The cottage leaves the palace far behind;
What is a lordling's pomp? a cumbrous load,
Disguising oft the wretch of human kind,
Studied in arts of hell, in wickedness refin'd!

O Scotia! my dear, my native soil!
For whom my warmest wish to Heaven is sent,
Long may thy hardy sons of rustic toil
Be blest with health, and peace, and sweet content!
And O may Heaven their simple lives prevent
From luxury's contagion, weak and vile;
Then howe'er crowns and coronets be rent,
A virtuous populace may rise the while,
And stand a wall of fire around their much-loved isle.

O Thou! who poured the patriotic tide,
That stream'd thro' Wallace's undaunted heart,
Who dared to nobly stem tyrannic pride,
Or nobly die, the second glorious part:
(The patriot's God peculiarly thou art,
His friend, inspirer, guardian, and reward!)
O never, never Scotia's realm desert;
But still the patriot, and the patriot-bard,
In bright succession raise, her ornament and guard!

AND A' THAT A' THAT
Is there, for honest Poverty
That hangs his head, an' a' that;
The coward slave--we pass him by,
We dare be poor for a' that!
For a' that, and a' that.
Our toils obscure an' a' that,

The rank is but the guinea stamp;
The Man's the gowd for a' that.

What though on hamely fare we dine,
Wear hoddin grey, and a that;
Gie fools their silks, and knaves their wine;
A Man's a Man for a' that:
For a' that, and a' that,
Their tinsel show, and a' that;
The honest man, tho' e'er sae poor,
Is king o' men for a' that.
Ye see yon birkie, ca'd a lord,
Wha struts, an' stares, an' a' that;
Tho' hundreds worship at his word,
He's but a coof for a' that:
For a' that, an' a' that,
His ribband, star, an' a' that:
The man o' independent mind
He looks an' laughs at a' that.

A prince can mak a belted knight,
A marquis, duke, an' a' that;
But an honest man's aboon his might,
Guid faith, he mauna fa' that!
For a' that, and a' that,
Their dignities and a' that;
The pith o' sense, an' pride o' worth,
Are higher rank than a' that.

Then let us pray that come it may,
(As come it will for a' that,)
That sense and worth, o'er a' the earth,
Shall bear the gree, an' a' that.
For a' that, and a' that,
It's coming yet for a' that,
That Man to Man, the warld o'er,
Shall brothers be for a' that.

HOLY WILLIE'S PRAYER.
O thou, wha in the heavens dost dwell,
Wha, as it pleases best thysel',

Sends ane to heaven, and ten to hell,
A' for thy glory,
And no for ony gude or ill
They've done afore thee!

I bless and praise thy matchless might,
Whan thousands thou hast left in night,
That I am here afore thy sight,
For gifts and grace,
A burnin' and a shinin' light
To a' this place.

What was I, or my generation,
That I should get sic exaltation,
I wha deserve sic just damnation,
For broken laws,
Five thousand years 'fore my creation,
Thro' Adam's cause.

When frae my mither's womb I fell,
Thou might hae plunged me in hell,
To gnash my gums, to weep and wail,
In burnin' lake,
Whar damned devils roar and yell,
Chain'd to a stake.

Yet I am here a chosen sample;
To show thy grace is great and ample;
I'm here a pillar in thy temple,
Strong as a rock,
A guide, a buckler, an example,
To a' thy flock.

But yet, O Lord! confess I must,
At times I'm fash'd wi' fleshly lust;
And sometimes, too, wi' warldly trust,
Vile self gets in;
But thou remembers we are dust,
Defil'd in sin.

O Lord! yestreen thou kens, wi' Meg

Thy pardon I sincerely beg,
O! may't ne'er be a livin' plague
To my dishonour,
An' I'll ne'er lift a lawless leg
Again upon her.

Besides, I farther maun allow,
Wi' Lizzie's lass, three times I trow
But Lord, that Friday I was fou,
When I came near her,
Or else, thou kens, thy servant true
Wad ne'er hae steer'd her.

Maybe thou lets this fleshly thorn,
Beset thy servant e'en and morn,
Lest he owre high and proud should turn,
'Cause he's sae gifted;
If sae, thy han' maun e'en be borne
Until thou lift it.

Lord, bless thy chosen in this place,
For here thou hast a chosen race:
But God confound their stubborn face,
And blast their name,
Wha bring thy elders to disgrace
And public shame.

Lord, mind Gawn Hamilton's deserts,
He drinks, and swears, and plays at carts,
Yet has sae mony takin' arts,
Wi' grit and sma',
Frae God's ain priests the people's hearts
He steals awa.

An' whan we chasten'd him therefore,
Thou kens how he bred sic a splore,
As set the warld in a roar
O' laughin' at us;--
Curse thou his basket and his store,
Kail and potatoes.

Lord, hear my earnest cry and pray'r,

Against the presbyt'ry of Ayr;
Thy strong right hand, Lord, mak it bare
Upo' their heads,
Lord weigh it down, and dinna spare,
For their misdeeds.

O Lord my God, that glib-tongu'd Aiken,
My very heart and saul are quakin',
To think how we stood groanin', shakin',
And swat wi' dread,
While Auld wi' hingin lips gaed sneakin'
And hung his head.

Lord, in the day of vengeance try him,
Lord, visit them wha did employ him,
And pass not in thy mercy by 'em,
Nor hear their pray'r;
But for thy people's sake destroy 'em,
And dinna spare.

But, Lord, remember me an mine,
Wi' mercies temp'ral and divine,
That I for gear and grace may shine,
Excell'd by nane,
And a' the glory shall be thine,
Amen, Amen!

TO A MOUSE, ON TURNING HER UP IN HER NEST WITH THE PLOUGH, NOVEMBER, 1785

Wee, sleekit, cow'rin, tim'rous beastie,
O, what a panic's in thy breastie!
Thou need na start awa sae hasty,
Wi' bickering brattle!
I wad be laith to rin an' chase thee,
Wi' murd'ring pattle!

I'm truly sorry man's dominion,
Has broken nature's social union,
An' justifies that ill opinion,
Which makes thee startle
At me, thy poor, earth-born companion,

An' fellow-mortal!

I doubt na, whiles, but thou may thieve;
What then? poor beastie, thou maun live!
A daimen-icker in a thrave
'S a sma' request;
I'll get a blessin wi' the lave,
An' never miss't!

Thy wee bit housie, too, in ruin!
It's silly wa's the win's are strewin!
An' naething, now, to big a new ane,
O' foggage green!
An' bleak December's winds ensuin,
Baith snell an' keen!

Thou saw the fields laid bare an' waste,
An' weary winter comin' fast,
An' cozie here, beneath the blast,
Thou thought to dwell,
Till crash! the cruel coulter past
Out-thro' thy cell.

That wee bit heap o' leaves an' stibble,
Has cost thee mony a weary nibble!
Now thou's turn'd out, for a' thy trouble,
But house or hald,
To thole the winter's sleety dribble,
An' cranreuch cauld!

But, Mousie, thou art no thy lane,
In proving foresight may be vain;
The best-laid schemes o' mice an 'men
Gang aft a-gley,
An'lea'e us nought but grief an' pain,
For promis'd joy!

Still thou art blest, compar'd wi' me
The present only toucheth thee:

But, Och! I backward cast my e'e.
On prospects drear!
An' forward, tho' I canna see,
I guess an' fear!

ADDRESS TO A HAGGIS
Fair fa' your honest, sonsie face,
Great chieftain o' the pudding-race!
Aboon them a' ye tak your place,
Painch, tripe, or thairm:
Weel are ye wordy o'a grace
As lang's my arm.

The groaning trencher there ye fill,
Your hurdies like a distant hill,
Your pin was help to mend a mill
In time o'need,
While thro' your pores the dews distil
Like amber bead.

His knife see rustic Labour dight,
An' cut you up wi' ready sleight,
Trenching your gushing entrails bright,
Like ony ditch;
And then, O what a glorious sight,
Warm-reekin', rich!

Then, horn for horn, they stretch an' strive:
Deil tak the hindmost! on they drive,
Till a' their weel-swall'd kytes belyve
Are bent like drums;
Then auld Guidman, maist like to rive,
Bethankit! hums.

Is there that o're his French ragout
Or olio that wad staw a sow,
Or fricassee wad make her spew
Wi' perfect sconner,
Looks down wi' sneering, scornfu' view
On sic a dinner?

Poor devil! see him owre his trash,
As feckles as wither'd rash,
His spindle shank, a guid whip-lash;
His nieve a nit;
Thro' bloody flood or field to dash,
O how unfit!

But mark the Rustic, haggis-fed,
The trembling earth resounds his tread.
Clap in his walie nieve a blade,
He'll mak it whissle;
An' legs an' arms, an' hands will sned,
Like taps o' thrissle.

Ye Pow'rs, wha mak mankind your care,
And dish them out their bill o' fare,
Auld Scotland wants nae skinking ware
That jaups in luggies;
But, if ye wish her gratefu' prayer
Gie her a haggis!

ADDRESS TO THE DEIL

O Thou! whatever title suit thee--
Auld Hornie, Satan, Nick, or Clootie,
Wha in yon cavern grim an' sootie,
Clos'd under hatches,
Spairges about the brunstane cootie,
To scaud poor wretches!

Hear me, auld Hangie, for a wee,
An' let poor damned bodies be;
I'm sure sma' pleasure it can gie,
Ev'n to a deil,
To skelp an' scaud poor dogs like me,
An' hear us squeal!

Great is thy pow'r an' great thy fame;
Far kenn'd an' noted is thy name;
An' tho' yon lowin' heuch's thy hame,
Thou travels far;
An' faith! thou's neither lag nor lame,

Nor blate, nor scaur.

Whyles, ranging like a roarin' lion,
For prey, a' holes and corners tryin;
Whyles, on the strong-wind'd tempest flyin,
Tirlin the kirks;
Whyles, in the human bosom pryin,
Unseen thou lurks.

I've heard my reverend grannie say,
In lanely glens ye like to stray;
Or where auld ruin'd castles grey
Nod to the moon,
Ye fright the nightly wand'rer's way,
Wi' eldritch croon.

When twilight did my grannie summon,
To say her pray'rs, douce, honest woman!
Aft yont the dyke she's heard you bummin,
Wi' eerie drone;
Or, rustlin, thro' the boortrees comin,
Wi' heavy groan.

Ae dreary, windy, winter night,
The stars shot down wi' sklentin light,
Wi' you, mysel' I gat a fright,
Ayont the lough;
Ye, like a rash-buss, stood in sight,
Wi' wavin' sough.

The cudgel in my nieve did shake,
Each brist'ld hair stood like a stake,
When wi' an eldritch, stoor "quaick, quaick,"
Amang the springs,
Awa ye squatter'd like a drake,
On whistlin' wings.

Let warlocks grim, an' wither'd hags,
Tell how wi' you, on ragweed nags,
They skim the muirs an' dizzy crags,
Wi' wicked speed;
And in kirk-yards renew their leagues,

Owre howkit dead.

Thence country wives, wi' toil and pain,
May plunge an' plunge the kirn in vain;
For oh! the yellow treasure's taen
By witchin' skill;
An' dawtit, twal-pint hawkie's gane
As yell's the bill.

Thence mystic knots mak great abuse
On young guidmen, fond, keen an' crouse,
When the best wark-lume i' the house,
By cantrip wit,
Is instant made no worth a louse,
Just at the bit.

When thowes dissolve the snawy hoord,
An' float the jinglin' icy boord,
Then water-kelpies haunt the foord,
By your direction,
And 'nighted trav'llers are allur'd
To their destruction.

An' aft your moss-traversin spunkies
Decoy the wight that late an' drunk is:
The bleezin, curst, mischievous monkies
Delude his eyes,
Till in some miry slough he sunk is,
Ne'er mair to rise.

When masons' mystic word an' grip
In storms an' tempests raise you up,
Some cock or cat your rage maun stop,
Or, strange to tell!
The youngest brither ye wad whip
Aff straught to hell.

Lang syne in Eden's bonie yard,
When youthfu' lovers first were pair'd,
An' all the soul of love they shar'd,
The raptur'd hour,
Sweet on the fragrant flow'ry swaird,

In shady bower;

Then you, ye auld, snick-drawing dog!
Ye cam to Paradise incog,
An' play'd on man a cursed brogue,
(Black be your fa'!)
An' gied the infant warld a shog,
'Maist rui'd a'.

D'ye mind that day when in a bizz
Wi' reekit duds, an' reestit gizz,
Ye did present your smoutie phiz
'Mang better folk,
An' sklented on the man of Uz
Your spitefu' joke?

An' how ye gat him i' your thrall,
An' brak him out o' house an hal',
While scabs and botches did him gall,
Wi' bitter claw;
An' lows'd his ill-tongu'd wicked scawl,
Was warst ava?

But a' your doings to rehearse,
Your wily snares an' fechtin fierce,
Sin' that day Michael did you pierce,
Down to this time,
Wad ding a Lallan tounge, or Erse,
In prose or rhyme.

An' now, auld Cloots, I ken ye're thinkin,
A certain Bardie's rantin, drinkin,
Some luckless hour will send him linkin
To your black pit;
But faith! he'll turn a corner jinkin,
An' cheat you yet.

But fare-you-weel, auld Nickie-ben!
O wad ye tak a thought an' men'!
Ye aiblins might--I dinna ken--
Stil hae a stake:
I'm wae to think up' yon den,

Ev'n for your sake!

TO A LOUSE, ON SEEING ONE ON A LADY'S BONNET, AT CHURCH

Ha! Wh'are ye gaun, ye crowlin ferlie?
Your impudence protects you sairly;
I canna say but ye strunt rarely,
Owre gauze and lace;
Tho', faith! I fear ye dine but sparely
On sic a place.

Ye ugly, creepin', blastit wonner,
Detested, shunn'd by saunt an' sinner,
How dare ye set your fit upon her--
Sae fine a lady?
Gae somewhere else and seek your dinner
On some poor body.

Swith! in some beggar's haffet squattle;
There ye may creep, and sprawl, and sprattle,
Wi' ither kindred, jumping cattle,
In shoals and nations;
Whaur horn nor bane ne'er dare unsettle
Your thick plantations.

Now haud you there, ye're out o' sight,
Below the fatt'rels, snug and tight;
Na, faith ye yet! ye'll no be right,
Till ye've got on it--
The verra tapmost, tow'ring height
O' Miss' bonnet.

My sooth! right bauld ye set your nose out,
As plump an' grey as onie grozet:
O for some rank, mercurial rozet,
Or fell, red smeddum !
I'd gie you sic a hearty dose o't,
Wad dress your droddum !

I wad na been surpris'd to spy
You on an auld wife's flannen toy;
Or aiblins some bit dubbie boy,

On's wyliecoat;
But Miss' fine Lunardi! fie!
How daur ye do't?

O Jenny, dinna toss your head,
An' set your beauties a' abroad!
Ye little ken what cursed speed
The blastie's makin:
Thae winks an' finger-ends, I dread,
Are notice takin'!

O wad some Pow'r the giftie gie us
To see oursels as others see us!
It wad frae mony a blunder free us,
An' foolish notion:
What airs in dress an' gait wad lea'e us,
An' ev'n devotion!

TO A GENTLEMAN WHO HAD SENT THE POET A NEWSPAPER AND OFFERED TO CONTINUE IT FREE OF EXPENSE

Kind Sir, I've read your paper through,
And faith, to me, 'twas really new!
How guessed ye, Sir, what maist I wanted?
This mony a day I've grain'd and gaunted,
To ken what French mischief was brewin;
Or what the drumlie Dutch were doin;
That vile doup-skelper, Emperor Joseph,
If Venus yet had got his nose off;
Or how the collieshangie works
Atween the Russians and the Turks,
Or if the Swede, before he halt,
Would play anither Charles the Twalt;
If Denmark, any body spak o't;
Or Poland, wha had now the tack o't:
How cut-throat Prussian blades were hingin;
How libbet Italy was singin;

If Spaniard, Portuguese, or Swiss,
Were sayin' or takin' aught amiss;
Or how our merry lads at hame,

In Britain's court kept up the game;
How royal George, the Lord leuk o'er him!
Was managing St. Stephen's quorum;
If sleekit Chatham Will was livin,
Or glaikit Charlie got his nieve in;
How daddie Burke the plea was cookin,
If Warren Hasting's neck was yeukin;
How cesses, stents, and fees were rax'd.
Or if bare arses yet were tax'd;
The news o' princes, dukes, and earls,
Pimps, sharpers, bawds, and opera-girls;
If that daft buckie, Geordie Wales,
Was threshing still at hizzies' tails;
Or if he was grown oughtlins doucer,
And no a perfect kintra cooser:
A' this and mair I never heard of;
And, but for you, I might despair'd of.
So, gratefu', back your news I send you,
And pray a' guid things may attend you.

Ellisland, Monday Morning, 1790.

AE FOND KISS
Ae fond kiss, and then we sever;
Ae fareweel, alas, for ever!
Deep in heart-wrung tears I'll pledge thee,
Warring sighs and groans I'll wage thee.

Who shall say that fortune grieves him,
While the star of hope she leaves him?
Me, nae cheerfu' twinkle lights me;
Dark despair around benights me.

I'll ne'er blame my partial fancy,
Naething could resist my Nancy:
But to see her was to love her;
Love but her, and love for ever.

Had we never lov'd sae kindly,
Had we never lov'd sae blindly,
Never met--or never parted,

We had ne'er been broken-hearted.

Fare-thee-weel, thou first and fairest!
Fare-thee-weel, thou best and dearest!
Thine be ilka joy and treasure,
Peace, Enjoyment, Love and pleasure!

Ae fond kiss, and then we sever!
Ae fareweel, alas, for ever!
Deep in heart-wrung tears I'll pledge thee,
Warring sighs and groans I'll wage thee.

ON THE BIRTH OF A POSTHUMOUS CHILD BORN IN PECULIAR CIRCUMSTANCES OF FAMILY DISTRESS

Sweet flow'ret, pledge o' meikle love,
And ward o' mony a prayer,
What heart o' stane wad thou na move,
Sae helpless, sweet, and fair?

November hirples o'er the lea,
Chil, on thy lovely form:
And gane, alas! the shelt'ring tree,
Should shield thee frae the storm.

May He who gives the rain to pour,
And wings the blast to blaw,
Protect thee frae the driving show'r,
The bitter frost and snaw.

May He, the friend o' Woe and Want,
Who heals life's various stounds,
Protect and guard the mother plant,
And heal her cruel wounds.

But late she flourish'd, rooted fast,
Fair in the summer morn,
Now feebly bends she in the blast,
Unshelter'd and forlorn.

Blest be thy bloom, thou lovely gem,

Unscath'd by ruffian hand!
And from thee many a parent stem
Arise to deck our land!

ELEGY ON THE YEAR 1788
For lords or kings I dinna mourn,
E'en let them die--for that they're born:
But oh! prodigious to reflec'!
A Towmont, sirs, is gane to wreck!

O Eighty-eight, in thy sma' space,
What dire events hae taken place!
Of what enjoyments thou hast reft us!
In what a pickle thou has left us!

The Spanish empire's tint a head,
And my auld teethless, Bawtie's dead:
The tulzie's sair 'tween Pitt and Fox,
An' our gudewife's wee birdy cocks;

The tane is game, a bludie devil,
But to the hen-birds unco civil;
The tither's something dour o' treadin,
But better stuff ne'er claw'd a middin.

Ye ministers, come mount the poupit,
An' cry till ye be hearse an' roupet,
For Eighty-eight, he wished you weel,
An' gied ye a' baith gear an' meal;
E'en mony a plack, and mony a peck,
Ye ken yoursels, for little feck!

Ye bonie lasses, dight your e'en,
For some o' you hae tint a frien';
In Eighty-eight, ye ken, was ta'en,
What ye'll ne'er hae to gie again.

Observe the very nowt an' sheep,
How dowff an' daviely they creep;
Nay, even the yirth itsel does cry,
For E'mbrugh wells are grutten dry.

O Eighty-nine, thou's but a bairn,
An' no owre auld, I hope, to learn!
Thou beardless boy, I pray tak care,
Thou now hast got thy Daddy's chair;
Nae handcuff'd, mizzl'd, hap-shackl'd Regent,
But, like himsel, a full free agent,
Be sure ye follow out the plan
Nae waur than he did, honest man!
As muckle better as you can.

January, 1, 1789.

ON SEEING A WOUND HARE LIMP BY ME WHICH A FELLOW HAD JUST SHOT AT

Inhuman man! curse on thy barb'rous art,
And blasted be thy murder-aiming eye;
May never pity soothe thee with a sigh,
Nor ever pleasure glad thy cruel heart!

Go live, poor wanderer of the wood and field!
The bitter little that of life remains:
No more the thickening brakes and verdant plains
To thee a home, or food, or pastime yield.

Seek, mangled wretch, some place of wonted rest,
No more of rest, but now thy dying bed!
The sheltering rushes whistling o'er thy head,
The cold earth with thy bloody bosom prest.

Perhaps a mother's anguish adds its woe;
The playful pair crowd fondly by thy side;
Ah! helpless nurslings, who will now provide
That life a mother only can bestow!

Oft as by winding Nith I, musing, wait
The sober eve, or hail the cheerful dawn,
I'll miss thee sporting o'er the dewy lawn,
And curse the ruffian's aim, and mourn thy hapless fate.

TO A RED RED ROSE

O my Luve's like a red, red rose,
That's newly sprung in June:
O my Luve's like the melodie,
That's sweetly play'd in tune.

As fair art thou, my bonie lass,
So deep in luve am I;
And I will luve thee still, my dear,
Till a' the seas gang dry.

Till a' the seas gang dry, my dear,
And the rocks melt wi' the sun;
And I will luve thee still, my dear,
While the sands o' life shall run.

And fare-thee-weel, my only Luve!
And fare-thee-weel, a while!
And I will come again, my Luve,
Tho' 'twere ten thousand mile!

EPITAPH ON HOLY WILLIE

Here Holy Willie's sair worn clay
Taks up its last abode;
His saul has taen some other way,
I fear, the left-hand road.

Stop! there he is, as sure's a gun,
Poor, silly body, see him;
Nae wonder he's as black's the grun,
Observe wha's standing wi' him.

Your brunstane devilship, I see,
Has got him there before ye;
But haud your nine-tail cat a wee,
Till ance you've heard my story.

Your pity I will not implore,

For pity ye have nane;
Justice, alas! has gien him o'er,
And mercy's day is gane.

But hear me, Sir, deil as ye are,
Look something to your credit;
A coof like him wad stain your name,
If it were kent ye did it.

SCOTS , WHA HAE

Robert Bruce's Address To His Army, Before The Battle Of Banockburn.

Scots, wha hae wi' Wallace bled,
Scots, wham Bruce has aften led,
Welcome to your gory bed
Or to victorie!

Now's the day, and now's the hour:
See the front o' battle lour,
See approach proud Edward's power -
Chains and slaverie!

Wha will be a traitor knave?
Wha will fill a coward's grave?
Wha sae base as be a slave? -
Let him turn, and flee!

Wha for Scotland's King and Law
Freedom's sword will strongly draw,
Freeman stand or freeman fa',
Let him follow me!

By oppression's woes and pains,
By your sons in servile chains,
We will drain our dearest veins
But they shall be free!

Lay the proud usurpers low!
Tyrants fall in every foe!

Liberty's in every blow!
Let us do or die!

AULD LANG SYNE
Should auld acquaintance be forgot,
And never brought to min?
Should auld acquaintance be forgot,
And auld lang syne!

For auld lang syne, my dear,
For auld lang syne.
We'll tak a cup o' kindness yet,
For auld lang syne.

We twa hae run about the braes,
And pou'd the gowans fine;
But we've wander'd mony a weary foot,
Sin' auld lang syne.

We twa hae paidled I' the burn,
From morning sun till dine;
But seas between us braid hae roar'd
Sin' auld lang syne.

And there's a hand, my trusty fiere!
And gie's a hand o' thine!
And we'll tak a right gude-willie waught,
For auld lang syne.

And surely ye'll be your pint stowp!
And surely I'll be mine!
And we'll tak a cup o'kindness yet,
For auld lang syne.